ghost composer

J. Dylan Yates

Chenery Pre

For information or permission requests, address Chenery Press Publishers at cheneryppress@gmail.com.

ISBN: 978-0-9963825-4-0 (E-Book)
ISBN: 978-0-9963825-5-7 (Paperback)

ghost composer
By J. Dylan Yates
I. Poetry

CHENERY PRESS published May 2026
Cover Art by Jann Nunn
Epigraph photo by Little Owl Productions
Cover Photo & Graphic Design by Lorie Tancredi-Baese
End Matter photo by Dylan Yates

PRINTED IN THE UNITED STATES OF AMERICA

Contents

Jaime, the most perfect body of water.

Natal

Your name day our first battleground. Holding you
inside, on my birth day. I kept you sheltered long
enough to gift you your own. Telling you,

Not yet.
We will separate.
You will have your own day.

You thrummed time against my gargling uterus
with your insistent heels. Two days
your poking fingers teased, until steak dinner at that

bleak sports bar. Your father and I interrupted by
a stab. Invisible tiny-iron-mace-stab into lumbar.
I gathered breath. Passenger manifest

now made public.
Time to release you from your water crib.
Wanting our privacy— a veil through this labour,

this production-of-mystical you, I stalled the hospital,
slithered home to gather birth supplies.
Through mace-burns, I remembered, three months

earlier, I'd had a natal dream—you and I, battling
birth. Just us, until a nurse came through a doorway
and asked your name. I shared the one you told me,

not the one I'd picked. You, insistent now, beat out
rhythms every three. At midnight, at hospital, nurse
told me

Go home.
No dilation.
Dr. prescribed me Seconal

Two weeks early.
Those pains are Braxton
Hicks.

Hiccups.
We are outnumbered.
I retreated from that battle, hobbled home,

took those pills, sleepy through that mace,
now grown anvil-hot,
my spine branded: Virago.

My mind strained
to sail away into a nameless country of
cease-fire.

No baby for two weeks.
Doctor ordered. At 4 a.m., I rocked into contractions.
Sweaty nightgown between my teeth to keep my

groans silent as your father slept. You struggled
lower. I woke your father—he, scared-cranky now,
called curt Doctor who said,

Let us all sleep.
I, exhausted, righteous, not meek now,
shouted at the phone,

If the Doctor won't deliver, I'll do it by myself.
I, now helpless, became a salt sailor.
Course uncharted,

steering into an ocean battleground of
roiling waves filled with flaming
weapons dealt on each contraction strike.

You chose that moment to break water. Doctor heard
transition sounds—those groans grown
agrestal.

Now, they translated.
Remorseful Doc instructed father—
        Usher her quickly.

Your father, on his crutches, not going anywhere with
haste. I crawled to the car myself.
At hospital, a wheelchair sweeps me to the elevator.

On the birth floor, same nurse loudly barks,
        Not ready for delivery.
        Two weeks early.

I, responding with the calm of chaos-certainty,
No.
Now.

After checking, nurse, all wounded with apology.
At eight centimeters, there was no epidural option.
I felt free and warriorlike

fighting for you.
Winning,
the 23-year-old me chanted.

Winning.
Forty-five minutes later, you silent and staring,
physical manifestation,

someone who had always been here with me.
On my ribs now, you lifted head and told me,
I am.

You were always the present

Hunger

The day you cried
on the way to Montessori school
and told me you had no friends

I asked why you felt that way
and talked you into going.
When we pulled up, several children

ran to the fence, chanting your name,
excited now that you
were there.

Look.
These are all your friends.
You smiled at them with such citrus surprise.

Your birthday parties—all the parties at our home
through the years—you worried no one would show
up. We barely had space for all your friends.

The linalool love spilled around our house.
Fragranced our walls. Could you feel it then,
or later at my last party for you? Your music school

graduation party. They came. They all came.
Family, friends, neighbors.
All of them, filled with limonene love for you.

For your talent. Your drive. For you.
You looked for encouragement from your uncles.
Mirrors in your cousins. You looked for

recognition—for the true nest of love.
That night, we stood in the kitchen, we washed dishes
together. I asked if you felt happy to see everyone,

and
you smiled.
Sweet.

You peeled an orange.
Its serotonin scent filled the kitchen
long after you'd gone up the stairs.

It filled the empty space
you left—
the uneaten orange

You Can Blow Out a Candle, but You Can't Blow Out a Fire

Your surprise present—
that red scooter you longed for.
My first big paycheck

bestowed on your sweetness.
We had your name printed on a card,
taped to that scooter in the store window.

Your eyes grew wide, at first stunned
by what you thought was coincidence.
Then, the delight

of knowing it was yours.
I loved building you endless magic,
but you came loaded, world's ago, in wisdom.

You sang all the words to Biko
And you knew it was a eulogy.
You rang meditation bells.

Those Backseat Buddha
statements echo from the car seat.
What's the secret of the world,

we asked you.
No hitting.

No pause taken, as if we all should know

Riding Shotgun

Remember when your first-grade teacher
failed to introduce that social-
services man present at the parent–teacher meeting,

held because your parents were young lesbians.
I think it must be hard on him.
What makes you think so?

You're being… different,
she answered.
That social services man, uncomfortable with

that chat,
apologized, excused himself, and left.
That teacher was fired after one year.

We lived in a neighborhood with a high number of
nannies per capita.
so, you must be the nanny?

I heard almost daily due to my youth and dress.
Remember the unprincipled principal who wouldn't
identify the parent who dragged you into school

by the neck, because he thought you'd taken his
child's shoe.
I'm pretty sure I frightened us all with

my quick and fiery temper,
about her incompetence, and ability to lead. She was
fired, years later, for inappropriate behavior with

her coworkers.
Remember your 7th-grade teacher
who said on your first day at a new school

that you were
going to be trouble.
For talking out of turn, she labeled you with titles you

hadn't earned yet, but you were comically proud
and eager to live up to. You were not the trouble.
She fled that roundtable parent meeting when I

brought it up. Your other teachers, silent.
Years later, I learned she choked a
student. Also fired.

The same me fights with your Canadian Doctor—
rolling, like the nursing task performed to keep your
skin

from degrading—degrading,
the way the neuro Doctors come
whenever I'm not there

In the Waiting Room

We collect minds.
Search intimation in photos,
music, tufts of hair, teeth, cuttings. Silent

in the company of those other parents,
those other friends, as we try to stop time. If I,
out of mind, panic, clutch stranger, strangle answers

from questions choked out that night,
it would be: if would have, should have,
Could we have?

Spiders crawl out of dingy corners.
We bow to hand sanitizers each time that corridor
door intercom demands names, ours, theirs,

prone patients mute, snuffed, accidents having.
One night, a tsunami threatens to wipe
all lower Victoria,

hospital, patients, waiting room, waiters.
Outside, it is pouring, and a violent storm rages. But
there is more destruction inside.

Gauzy sacrifices made, stoic put aside and gathered
secretly again. Band-aid pacts. Thaumaturgy.
Impossibilities. Those dimming, aged fluorescents.

We cannot see each other in this space. Silent.
Spin, pray, pause, relentlessly breathe,
and You, God, the sly remote,

crouching in the corner easy chair.
As less of us tapped knees during the waiting, we
could ask to be forgiven.

We could blame, confess, could search for absolution
elsewhere than on sick colored,
mustard-smelling, sticky counters.

Walls,
Paint,
The burnt coffee

hope abiding in that room.
The reckoning. The wee, spiked hammers
we conceived behind our eyes

Water Under Skin

1.

You summoned me on this long commute.
Remote. Living on an island in our blood you found
around the age I fled mine.

My tiny-frozen-broken finger, Hull, leading to your
rain garden Victoria.

Your wanderings, no doubt, led by cells we share
(yours travel in my body, too), landed us both just
above the US, on a strand of familiar land.

DNA-determined architecture—environment.
Although, gene expression subsequently altered—
perhaps it was an Epigenetic Settlement.

Soft, quiet. I knelt by your bed and fell back. Both
men—your father, your friend— moved swiftly to
support what could not be supported.

2.

Time began its warp.
I banished bleak conversations into the hallway.
Doctors, nurses, father, friends, night crew. All.

Not in this room.
Not while you listened.
Although you heard my weakness.

Your blinks of exhaustion after coma—
after medication titrated to bring you to our present.
After seizure.

One blink for yes, two blinks for no. Or was it one
blink for no? It doesn't matter to the Doctor, who
insists she must dismiss the blinking.

It's not reproducible.
The music tears, the blood-pressure-spiked-responses,
the turn of your head to my voice.

You cannot see, but your eyes track sound reflexively,
encouraging belief and hope. Your blinks at your
father: perceived abandonment anger;

your other mother, the gathering Calypso nymph;
a version of the legend told from your perspective,
the thief who stole my father.

3.

The nurses; the processional of medical detail;
the ICU bed, the table, the chairs, the desk, the
computer, the O2, the vent,

the blood pressure, the hope that mounts;
the nighttime cleaning crew, in their gray scrubs.
The mop, the pail on wheels. These cannot be kept

sterile in that room. You cannot be kept sacred
in that room. Pneumonia inevitable with this loss of
reverence. Bacteria swirled around those white

countertops, the equipment, the tubing, the IVs, the
despair.
Your eyes, blinking.

I played old music—your music—and your seizures
start again.
Irony in the midst of panic.

That was your reaction, too, to my
electric music, Mom.
Your House, Dub, Drum and Bass, Glitch Hop.

All those years I called it
white boys on speed.
I teased you. Now I hear it. I can hear you in it,

moving me on an unsentimental level to my core.
Finally, I understand it takes pure stillness,
not speed, to really listen.

It is the left evidence,
the coherent effect of
your music in my cells

Binaural

You: Still. Peaceful.
Vitals stable. You breathe
in half-time, letting the respirator do the rest.

Blinking back under, you begin your sound
performance, your body turns to my voice
—an aural tease.

My laptop in the hospital; rhythm's beat through
walls, the floors, your body now turning to
familiar music. The music floats with gamma-wave

intention, supplicant, to heal your brain.
Your face never showing,
us never knowing exactly who,

how, what,
where you're going.
Absent movement in your legs and arms.

Sight-blinded.
Your brain wired for sound in
every non-aural area from

so many nights and days of EDM neuronal patterning
in that Chinatown apartment. Those Fan Tan
Alley opium ancestors must have

laughed, most likely cowered, terrified,
desperate to make that noise from the
future cease.

Don't touch.
Too much stimulation for him.
Yet, when I squeeze your hand, you squeeze mine

in perfect rhythm.
Perfect.
The same rhythmic conversation we had holding

hands when you were little.
Do you love me? *Yes I do.*
How much? *More than birds can tell.*

Reflex,
says your Doctor, with a profile we've exhumed,
volunteers in Africa each year.

Shall we trust her?
Blink once for yes, two for no
She's not a neuro doc, just a General

giving orders—commander intent.
The day the Doctor ushers us
into the consult lounge—you, binaural blinking

in the other room.
His neuro tests show steady APGAR scores.
We want to see improvement.

We should improve the nurse who scrapes the skin
under your nails to test pain. Decorticate repelled.
Your body, the only language the medical staff can

interpret. Your posture doesn't speak intention.
We should improve another's impassive response to
tube-feed gag aspiration. She should

read her textbooks
again. Forgive me.
We had a deal.

When I died, I would float a feather horizontal.
Like Lennon.
You would be here on the earth for that.

Dealbreaker

Never Letting Go

The Doctor argued that I did not need to see an MRI
of your hypoxic brain—the proof highlighted in
contrast.

Your mysterious, brilliant
brain sleeping in the auditory
cortex, yet wired for sound

in parts those neuro nerds
thought compelling enough to keep you breathing—
granting breath.

That mechanical tube a prop in your halftime show.
Tease, when you opened your eyes and spoke a
blinked language.

Were you were still thinking,
                                        Asses,
when they ushered us into a lounge to make

decisions?
(Feeding tube v. aspiration pneumonia,
medication v. incanting clarity through pain),

as if will had reason, as if
decisions would ever be anything but acid-burned
tattoos

projected strobe-like in the hippocampus.
My optic chiasma exchanging strands of genetic
material set to glitch-hop.

We spoke around you, through you, and ourselves,
and the nurses.
Reticulated hope.

You, listened from your bed, thinking,
Asses.
Me, in my out, negotiating chaos. Your father

parroted Doctors.
All your mothers. Apologies. Forgiveness.
We all tried.

It was like one long, depressing,
dysfunctional,
Thanksgiving Day

After Days of Gag Aspiration

in not a moment of despair,
but hope,
I decide to have your feeding tube

removed.
Vitals stable. Seizures hidden.
Stomach put on pain reprieve.

Your medicine cabinet
crowded with antacids since your twenties.
I expected you to chew your food in the

coming days. How could I have been
so naïve, forgetting
hospital directives.

The subtext message sent to staff

We Could Have Had a Banquet on the Words

tethered to your eyelids.
The tears you cried at Sara's song,
the only

concrete conversation
we could carve for Doctors.
How we raged within those white walls, you and I,

at the unaddressed hunger—the thirst.
I finally said no to the monitors and tubes,
the respiratory therapist's violent tendings.

I would have kidnapped you,
gauze-bound on a plane for Kauai or
somewhere light had color in it.

That morning, after tsunami warnings and hurricanes,
a rainbow foretold your future.
We all felt it.

You, in your still,
eyes closed
and listening

Ghost Composer

You always drew a crowd of separate Worlds—
sometimes left them rattled and shambolic.
Maybe it was just my bones confused.

Most left smiling in your wake.
You found happiness coded in a perfect chord—
always in the present of your melodic beat.

Your suppressed genetic coding
kept that *will-cell* un-transcribed.
I'll carry that, bear the fault—

imperfection. That early-life loss lesson,
hidden in milky chocolate,
sweetened up and sectioned;

board games played in 90mph winds.
Dinosaurs grazed grass on hung wallpaper
oblivious to the asteroids that threatened—

before mass extermination;
vibrant colors constant, canvas stretched already
for your illumination variation—all the dark

adaptation. As though grey would harvest souls.
From first to last, each scene was set to music;
And then the world without the plastic coating;

all the chocolate melted in your hands.
No pause, no sleep, against the damage dealt
by Roar of Time. Numb fear

at the thresholds of those endless doorways
to the expansive world. You agonized with the
offerings. *Trust the red pill or the blue.*

Really can't, really don't, really won't
understand why you left
in the middle of your set

Extubation

You relaxed and breathed easily at first:
Your father, and other mother, overcome,
wrung-exhausted by your endurance,

retreated.
Long ago, on those court-ordered parental visits,
you weren't ready for that push and pull.

At 15, when you chose to know your father,
first living like a stranded immigrant in his cold,
Canadian basement.

You had already found your first taste of chemical
freedom. You wanted out of childhood when you
stepped into the Raves,

and drugs and booze and downtown apartments.
Yet you still needed navigational embrace—the coded
secret to the safe.

For days (and years), you survived without that
breathing tube.
You were obviously raised by women warriors.

You survived that.
You survived those mistakes
and mine

There in the night, the night I rang

and asked the nurse if you were awake,
were you listening
to hospital sounds? The cleaning crew?

grace?
Were you leaning into life? Making deals?
Erasing doubts? Greeting dead friends?

There was an invocation in that space

Juliets

1.
So many young women
threw themselves
on your Sleeping Prince chest—

like reverent Juliets, grieving,
the lifesaving, secret message
lost along the way. After one day

of shared tears—those women,
younger and younger,
the days that followed brought

levity with each deathbed scene.
You loved generously.
Evidently.

2.
Hospital switchboards jammed for your visit
appointments. At end of day another young
woman sits by your bed

in quietude, devotedly,
until I ask how she knows you.
She admits

she doesn't know you, personally.
A Follower, a Critical groupie.
It was clear it was

time to shut the whole thing down.
You'd had enough
Juliet's, letters, songs, egg apologies, and substance

tributes. I should mention your friend collapsing with
the therapeutic K at your bedside,
the nurses bringing

pillows for his head on that hospital floor.
Canadian comfort.
I'm certain you were smiling and tired, too.

It was closing time

Something Shifted in the Distance

before they wheeled us off to the Blue Room,
that final space, a spirit-quilted comfort
of ironic morphine as you lifted onwards.

Those last breaths to drums only you could hear,
only you could feel,
in those eternal DJ Jungle Rooms.

Towards the end, you traveled briefly
from the space in the Blue Room.
I felt you go and return.

Visiting girlfriends.
Greeting dead grandpas.
Summoning your absent father.

It was hard to listen to you, and it
wasn't, each breath a
snoring possibility,

every
sound—
agonic promise

You Were Always Washing Dishes for Penance

No coincidence
you became the Master Dishwasher
in your Chinatown.

I have a memory—you skateboarding
on the Great Sand Dunes. Sliding, skidding, making
some advance,

then simply abandoning the board—jumping into air.
The air, your last debate on the edge of life.
The element you craved.

Forever,
you tried to tattoo on your chest in binary code.
You shared that tattoo with someone loved—

someone who loved you
so much she didn't tell you binary code F
was the only letter you both managed to grit through.

Then a little accident, Those Bits of You Falling Out of Box

You could not be contained.
First, tipping from your wooden urn
into the backpack I inherited.

Then blowing everywhere—
in hair, on pants,
on sea rocks.

After scatter
I took a taste of you.
You melted on my tongue, like a salty snowflake.

There were so many places I wanted to be with you.
Now I bring your backpack for travel—
bits of you: bone to ash to wood

to plastic vinyl. I carry you,
your dust, with me this way.
You could not stay central to that sea inlet.

Your constant friends, the winds, the currents.
Will I find you when I want another taste?
The decision to be there—

at Clover Point—both of us.
When you showed me, I said,
I'd like to be scattered here.

You bringing *me* to that windy watergrave.
A view we shared through cells. Psychic boy.
You were foretelling checkpoint failures.

Parts will travel on that Pacific—
communal.
In water—on a craft-less cruise.

You, your grandfather—
there you both are in the Pacific,
obligate resprouters

regenerating
in the
undertow

Hospital Nightmare Perseverative Parade

Still here.

Those juggling clowns all crowding into the tiny car.
Those marching bands of black-robed priests.

The hospital chaplain waving as he passes.
That donor rep, spinning clipboards filled with paper
failure. The Doctor waving from a red convertible,

her pretty baby balanced on a shoulder.
The nurses file, solemn, bearing hospital banners
listing protocol.

One for each day of your staying and passing.
No visitors after 9PM.
No visitors during vent flushing.

No visitors during change of shift report.
No visitors during tube cleanings.
No visitors during patient hygiene.

No scream. No blame. No questions.
No explanations. No film. No touch.
No hope. No rage. No breath.

The cleaning crew with mops and wheeled pails
perform a roaming dance—
cryptically choreographed. The receptionists I knew

by name at end of two-week residency,
single file, all smiles and
pointing to the sky

Visitation and Memento

Ethereal gifts of grief relief—
brief metaphysical
occupations.

A slant of butter sunlight
frames the photo-booth souvenir.
On the dining chair leg,

I find your wood-grain profile
in relief.
The pool

trembles a ghostly reflection
on the pure-white glossy ceiling.
Lights flutter, lights blink off.

Twice at 3 AM, a living room downlight
crashes on.
Tiny white feathers

float across the empty,
and land like alien craft
offerings.

Then, one day they fall silently and blanket our front
lawn, those white feathers.
Overkill.

Comic emphasis.
Night I wake to find
your friend's astounding,

gutting poetry-slam eulogy
grace Facebook during the Live minutes
it appeared and disappeared.

Night I conjured Gmail password in a dream.
Day I spend invading your privacy—
forensick.

Messages you deliver me about contacting people you
care for, people you want me to know—you have an
accomplished crowd.

Your finished and unfinished music found on
hard drives. Singing background vocals.
You whisper to me on those tracks: listen here.

Music so far out of your genre,
and killing it.
Hush, Sugar Nightclub, Spice Lounge,

Sevilla, Cadiz, Malaga, DJ posters arrive
in cardboard tubes at our doorstep,
like nightclub descendants finally immigrating.

Beatport, Soundcloud, music-chart-climbing
screen shots. Pictures you saved,
pictures you hid.

I shuffle a bit.
Did you seek balance at the edge of that crane you
tightroped at the Johnson bridge construction site?

Or was it flight

The Spring Break We Had Our Best Road Trip

Banning others from our duo plan,
we traveled to the Western Slope but missed our
mark.

A dance of missed surprise connections, she,
the girl we planned to visit, now in our space
back on the Front Range, us in hers.

We picked her for us on that trip,
marveling at her T-shirts, folded like a retail store, in
baby-blue milk bins lining the wall. We called her to

guess where we were, laughing when we told her we
were in her bed. Both of us falling deeper, dreaming
of a time to make our wish come true.

Continuing on our journey to those Four Corners,
volcanic lands, Ouray Hot Spas, we belted Melissa
Indigo tunes. We drove stalwart through a storm,

while my cold cleared and threw wishes into Grand
Canyons. I asked you to make a list of ten wants.
You complied, with your full list for world betterness.

1.) End of global hunger
2.) Peace, and so on.

I prompted,

one for you.
You thought for a long time and finally wrote:
A Super Nintendo.

I shared that story with your distant grandmother.
She bought it for you then, months earlier
than your 8th birthday.

I loved her for that.
That story is you—the only child I've known
who needed prompting to be selfish.

Essence in one gesture.
We sailed those bits of paper dreams
into far-reaching spaces to decompose and seed,

before a blizzard caused a reroute of our plan
to backtrack and ink the deal with that girl.
But we had Santa Fe for consolation.

You, standing by that statue on the plaza.
Us, shopping for
refrigerator magnets.

We have so much joy
bonded
between us

If I want, I can remember most of it

There's the wedding
we crashed during a Bar-Mitzvah
at that Vail hotel, swing-dancing wildly.

In our Kia, we slid backward in terror, down
the icy hill at your art instructor's home.
Hang on!

At the bottom I asked,
Are you OK?
You smiled at me.   *Can we do it again?*

Top of Estes Mountain, totally exhausted,
we water-toasted our success and glee-screamed
as we coasted all the way back down.

Go-kart laps, giant slides on magic carpets,
Elitch Gardens rollercoaster rides.
Your childhood went

faster than all the speed
we tried to gather.
Our best summer waking up together—

Devil's Gulch Cabin
white noise river lulled your latent sleep.
Your favorite home—

an interlude of wooden-walkway-condo,
pool at the bottom of our stairwell.
You wore a lifejacket all day,

every day, those sweet summers, for my anxiety.
Craving dive freedom with that float shackle.
One morning, you shared your dream.

You dreamed of breathing underwater.
                                        I'll never drown, Mom.
Life jacket tossed,

under neighbors' watch.
Shallow bottom scraped.
A red bolt curved down

your pretty forehead, pretty nose, for months.
Always, always diving pearls.
Gondolier Spaghetti Wednesdays.

Good Times twice a week. We had
schedules taped to our refrigerator with all the free
kids' meals offered every weeknight in that city,

and I worked five jobs arranged around
your school schedule to pay the bills.
But we were free and joyous.

Nothing came between us then but Sushi Zan Mai.
You gobbled eel treats, made by Maki-San,
who often played his sax, behind the counter, for you.

You ate every fish creation at 6 years. Charming
Itamae, who fed you mountains of green-tea ice
cream. In your teens, when you traveled to Japan,

was it the Japanese gene expressions we shared, or
were you learning Kanji from those menus?
Storing languages, like pencils we found in your

bedroom heat register. Your brain, collecting
all the Latins like Pokéman cards you bought
from an importer, then sold for profit

on an online site called E-Bay.
Mystifying me with your enterprises, like the words
you spoke from highchairs—only registering with

repetition and your patient illustrations.
Dancing with a belly dancer, you stole every show,
Bambi-lash magnet. You forced me to rescue every

crawly creature or risk a repeat of your toddler
meltdown, the Beetle Squashing Incident. You
taught me connection on the level you were living.

Always teaching me. Hiking Mt. Sanitas after school.
The cat you named Flash, following you, Sherpa-like,
on those trails. Flash,

sleeping on your head, first sleep to his last.
Chautauqua picnics. The bike races, the foot races,
my heart races when I think these things.

You speak me a gentle reprimand,
a bitter truth,
a kind word about the thing I couldn't

comfort

You—Born of a Human Divining Rod and Coded for Water

Since gone, you've missed:
Most of the worst President in history—
the one you foretold would be elected

from your sibylline Canada perch.
Your dear friends' wedding—
the ones you introduced to each other.

The birth of their boy—
sweet joy at seeing more love blossom.
But, also your best friend's sudden death.

A blind pandemic—
moveable Tetris minefields of warnings.
A moment where the

entire globe experienced the distinct,
zeitgeist awareness of our existential anxiety.
This opportunity to change our lives—

to break free and challenge all the hard rules,
the silly mores, mean injustices—
the plans our parents dreamed for them through us.

The Zombie mink that surfaced post-Covid-burial—
as I knew you would, had we not burned
your body and spread it direct in a water grave

At Birth is Mammalian Instinct, Infant Staring Intently

Memorizing iris patterns, babies
pick out mothers in crowds of hundreds
with that first gaze. Every mammal.

We breathe first breaths into makers' mouths.
You gave me that. (You gave me so much.)
Yours was the gaze of a wise old man.

Would you pick me again?
I drew third-eye circles on your forehead
as your heart slowed, *There are so many people*

waiting to see you.
You are so loved.
You sighed and started out, a driver now,

I swept the air past
your brain, your body,
that periwinkle comforter.

While you, still, gazed into my eyes,
that same old man gaze, then exhaled one last breath
into mine,

and made your final way
                    onward,
your way   *forward*

Celebration of Life 1.0

Written by Christopher (Yeti) Springbett
August 26th,1982 - February 10th, 2020

This has been my first experience with the passing of someone so close to me, and I was wholly unprepared for the seemingly endless void that formed right here in the pit of my stomach. A hole which I have carried with me everywhere I go, every minute, of every day. I've been told that time heals all wounds, but that with grief like this, even as it does, no matter how much time passes the slightest, seemingly insignificant, detail could trigger a memory that brings it right back again – it never truly goes away, it just gets easier. But the truth is, much as it hurts, I don't want it to go away. I dunno; maybe I'm just not ready yet... But I've also been struck by the physical representation of another emotion. Love. Right here, feeling like it's ready to burst right out of my chest. Sitting on top of that pit in my stomach - an emotional counterbalance.

Jaime was reliably focused; there's no question about that. He wasn't just chasing a dream; he was actively living it. Had been since the day I met him. He worked so hard on something he loved so much and clawed ahead, making progress by the hour, day, month, year... Never a second thought. We're talking about someone who, over a decade later, achieved a goal he'd set out for himself when he was twelve. I'm sure I had goals when I was twelve, but I'll be damned if I can remember what they were, and I certainly never followed through on any of them. His passions were consuming in the ways that nurture true genius. He had an incredible talent, but not just an innate gift. Jaime was a rare example of what happens when natural gifts meet hard work and a level of dedication that most of us will never know. That's passion. That was Jaime. Just try and get those headphones off his head.

Recently, we've gotten a glimpse into just how many lives he touched and how many people cared for him so deeply. If I had a regret, it would be that he didn't get to see this incredible outpouring of love and support. But I don't have any regrets. I know he knew it; he always did, and he always will. Certainly, there was something very special inside him that bonded us all so closely, though, if I'm going to be completely honest, I think part of it might have been those Bambi eyelashes of his.

Which is to say, that we all loved him the first time we laid eyes on him. That that love has endured so long, spread so far, and remained so strong is a testament to his character, one I will forever aspire to emulate. The character, not the lashes… He was tenacious, fearless, and endlessly curious. His empathy was like a law of physics – a gravitational force that pulled people to him. He often met total strangers who would tell him deeply personal and often tragic stories. He didn't know those people, but they felt safe with him. Though I can't put words to it, I think we all know why they did. He listened. He helped where he could with what little he had, but, more importantly, he listened. He carried their tragedies on his shoulders because… Because that's who he was. Those people were strangers – I don't have to tell anyone here the lengths he would go to for a friend.

The stories he shared with me shone a light not just on his empathy but his curiosity as well. They seemed random and unconnected at first, but as a pattern of extremity began to emerge, I came to realize that he wanted to see and experience everything. He carried the good with the bad. That's what it means to experience everything. That's one of many things that he taught me.

Writing this was hard for me, cathartic, but hard. Though I found most of what I've said flowed easily and naturally from my mind to the page, it's the end that I've struggled with – even struggled with that very word "end." Maybe there's just been too much finality in our lives already, or maybe there's just too much too to say – how many words would it take to truly honour such a beautiful and complex person? How do you translate the evolution of so many years of love and friendship to the page?

Intro/Verse/Buildup/Drop/Breakdown/ Outro

On January 26th, 2018, our son, Jaime, died. He was thirty-three years old.

This is a story that parents don't want to hear. This is a story we want to avoid any connection to. But this is a story that parents *must* listen to so that we can genuinely support and help our children overcome the enormous challenges and destruction that a substance-use disorder can cause. In writing these pieces of Jaime's story, I hope to humanize what is dehumanizing. Substance-Use Disorder is one of the most misunderstood and stigmatized health conditions. That stigma, with the myths that perpetuate it, is probably the biggest barrier to successful treatment due to the fear of community judgment.

Nothing prepared us for the battle we waged. We were, at once, misled, uneducated, and unsupported. Hindsight informs me that it wasn't shocking that Jaime couldn't manage his addiction. It was a miracle he lived as long as he did, managing an untreated disease by himself.

After a year of unearthing Jaime's history, before we had the cause of his death explained in detail and validated, I had gathered enough information about my son's adult life to absorb and begin to process the truth of his passing.

For the last six months of his life, Jaime was taking prescribed Xanax, a benzodiazepine, to manage his anxiety and help him sleep. Over the fifteen years of his music career and work history, Jaime had developed a pattern of sleep deprivation that became increasingly challenging as he aged. He struggled for years to sleep more than four or five hours at a time while trying to maintain a music career, hold down other jobs, and attend school.

But after his prescription ran out, Jaime bought his Xanax from a dealer. In the months before he died, Jaime told me himself that street drugs of any kind were especially risky in Victoria, because, increasingly, everything was being cut with Fentanyl.

The last pill Jaime took, late on Friday night, January 12th, 2018, was laced with a lethal dose of Fentanyl. He was in his favorite bakery in Chinatown, enjoying a piece of chocolate cake, when he ingested the pill and almost immediately went down. He was subsequently hospitalized. After a two-week rollercoaster of hopeful recovery signs and then ominous setbacks, he passed.

The only information we obtained from the initial hospital report was that he had a "few drugs" in his system in various forms and amounts, including Benzodiazepine (Xanax) and Fentanyl. Jaime's cause of death was initially labeled Severe Anoxic Injury due to Accidental Multiple Drug Intoxication. The hospital was unable to verify the substances in his system until the results of a venous blood drug test.

The presence of those drugs was simply a forensic fact in the hospital report. For us, it created more confusion, frustration, becoming yet another mysterious element of his death. From the moment he lost consciousness in the bakery until the moment he passed two weeks later, Jaime was unable to tell us what had happened as he was intubated and non-verbal. But I do not believe that he was consistently unconscious, as he responded with head turns, grasp reflex, and eye blinks to the sound of my voice, touch, and the music we played for him.

As a result, we had many questions, so we collected hair samples to help us piece together the truth. We sent the lock of hair we snipped from Jaime at his bedside to a lab in San Diego for sample testing. After months, the results returned, offering concrete answers yet raising new questions.

It took almost a year for us to receive the coroner's report and learn precisely what had happened to cause Jaime's death because the British Columbia Police and the Coroner's office were so inundated and overwhelmed with drug cases.

It was agony to lose our son; it became torture for us not to have the answers we needed to begin to process the loss. I started an intensive search to learn more about my son's life. What I learned, with the help of his friends, ultimately led all of us to profound discoveries. After he passed, we also heard many stories of his propensity for curious exploration and behavioral extremes in treacherous arenas, including his substance use.

Jaime was a musician. Drug and alcohol misuse in the music industry is not only rampant; it has been condoned and even encouraged by the accepted industry pattern of paying musicians with alcohol and illegal substances. As a result, the fact that Jaime had a substance-use disorder was not surprising. We were aware of his challenge after the age of twenty-six, when he began to share it.

Before that time, Jaime had been adept at hiding the severity of his illness from us, and still, he was not entirely forthcoming in his disclosure. He repeatedly, and vehemently, denied his drug use, telling us that he never used drugs, that his disorder was solely alcohol related. After he passed, his friends also shared a surprising fact with us. He would clean up physically and cease his substance use when we visited together. He held jobs, sometimes for years; he produced and distributed volumes of music; he went to school; he had intimate relationships, and he seemed to be maintaining his responsibilities at work and in his life. While it was becoming clear that he had additional mental health challenges, a co-occurring disorder of some kind, without sobriety, an accurate diagnosis was impossible.

Still, my wife and I are both RN's... we *should* have recognized all the signs, but, until the last years of Jaime's life, we believed that his disease was limited in its scope. How could he be keeping such a severe problem a secret from us?

Most frustratingly, substance-use disorder is in my family's disease history. I was literally raised in an environment that should have trained me more precisely to recognize the illness, and my early years of Alanon attendance *should* have been instructive for me, giving me additional insight and direction. The whole truth is that I believed exactly what I wanted to believe.

What we didn't realize was that the challenges Jaime shared with us were just the tip of the iceberg. The severity of his addiction was far below the surface presented; its depth, at times, accumulating, while at the same time eventually eroding and disappearing his being.

This loss, this kind of anticipatory grief, is its own kind of pain. When a loved one begins to lose connection to themselves due to substance use, it is one of the most difficult human experiences. So many of the people I work with share a similar, excruciating process and history before the ultimate loss of their loved one.

What is also, too often, a common throughline for those whose lives are lost is a rare sensitivity, or artistry, in one way or another, that is shared among the folks who use substances as self-medicating buffers to life's pain. In adding this fact, I do not wish to further romanticize the "tortured artist" trope. Self-destruction is not a by-product or catalyst for artistic genius. The lore ignores the fatal reality of addiction. Every life lost to a substance-use disorder is its own tragedy for every reason imaginable.

As a child, it was clear that Jaime was remarkable. At age two, he had an extraordinary vocabulary and enjoyed long conversations with almost everyone he met. Jaime began showing an evident talent for music by the age of four. We enrolled him in piano and percussion lessons, and he began composing his own music.

Jaime's sensitive nature became increasingly evident. His first-grade teacher shared that she had never known a child his age to be as compassionate. The eulogies delivered by his friends were filled with stories of his many kindnesses, not only for his friends, but often for complete strangers, his love for animals (including the raccoons that frequented his neighborhood), and his keen devotion to helping others through difficult times. Jaime cultivated loving relationships with people from highly diverse backgrounds. He was an extraordinary listener.

Besides a capacity to learn and play music, and a talent for drawing, languages came easily to him; by age 15, he had studied French, German, Spanish, and Japanese. This led to the opportunity to spend a summer on a cultural exchange tour in Japan. That summer was followed by a move to his father's home on Vancouver Island, BC, where he hoped to develop a closer relationship with his Canadian family.

Jaime began a successful musical career at 17, playing clubs and venues in Victoria, BC. He built his in-home music studio in an old, decrepit Chinatown building adjacent to Fan Tan Alley, where he lived for over a decade. He bargained for tech parts online and repurposed computers, keyboards, and other equipment to create his own studio. That studio eventually became a generative space for him to dream, develop, and grow musically.

But Jaime struggled throughout his years of success, even with the happiness he found in creating and playing music. Ultimately, he became unable to manage his life due to his substance-use disorder as well as a series of brain injuries from multiple falls. Ironically, maybe magically, he managed to fulfill some of his greatest life goals even as he began the difficult task of working toward sobriety.

In April 2015, Jaime won a full scholarship to a music school and moved to Vancouver, BC, to pursue video and post-game music production. While at school, he continued recording and producing his own music and engineering for many other musicians. He also volunteered his talents, composing music for a start-up video game company.

In February of 2017, after his graduation, Jaime moved into an apartment in a Vancouver suburb, and in March of 2017, he began a new job with Microsoft, engineering sound for the video game Gears of War. These experiences were penultimate achievements; he expressed happiness and gratitude for these opportunities. Jaime seemed very focused on his new career trajectory.

At the same time, his struggle to stay sober and manage his new life intensified. What we learned through my 'forensick' searches, and the hair sample taken at the hospital, which exposed his drug use for the last four months of his life, was heartbreaking and startling. The hair sample revealed what Jaime never admitted to anyone, including his girlfriends and his best friends. He managed to hide something completely and devastatingly disastrous for him.

Besides the prescription Xanax, Jaime had been using one other drug quite regularly. Ketamine. I eventually learned he'd been using street Ketamine, sometimes daily, for at least three years, perhaps longer. As Jaime shared before he passed, street Ketamine is now almost always cut with small amounts of Fentanyl. I've had a knock-down, drag-out with my feelings about Ketamine. I believe that in its prescribed pharmaceutical form, Ketamine has therapeutic possibilities for some patients. The way Jaime had been taking it ultimately proved fatal. The path Jaime took, which led to its lethality, was perhaps not as direct as most would assume, and yet the destination was seemingly inevitable.

My greatest hope is that sharing Jaime's life story will inspire and connect families and friends around the issues of substance-use disorder. My intention is to expand understanding around the need for early intervention. We've learned a great deal about substance-use disorders in the years since Jaime's passing and acknowledge there is much more to learn.

Also, I have a passionate mission. There are two substance-use myths I would like to see busted forever.

One: Recovery requires a person to "hit bottom" first. The reality is that this hazardous myth can prevent early intervention, which has been shown to lead to better outcomes. Seek help early and often.

Two: There is a fallacy in treatment that to effectively treat someone who has an alcohol/drug problem, you need to use something called “tough love.” Unfortunately, methods such as threatening someone with consequences for not changing their behavior or forcing them out of their home do not seem very effective at helping the person recover; in fact, they can have the opposite effect, making a person feel more ashamed and alone after experiencing such consequences. Addiction is not a moral failure; it is a chronic illness that creates feelings of being unlovable and hopeless in persons with addictions.

Enabler is the damaging label often given to someone who is simply caring for a loved one—providing food, safety, or housing—yet this care is not only necessary, it offers crucial support and is often a pathway to recovery. I feel grateful to have rejected the label “enabler” and refused to let the term affect my care for Jaime when it was used to describe our relationship. In doing so, I have fewer regrets amidst the many mistakes I made along the way. However, I feel a deep sadness that I hid my support for Jaime from everyone, even my wife, for years. It created more shame and isolation for Jaime and for me.

Using behavior modification techniques, EMDR, other trauma-based modalities, and creating healthy, loving boundaries, along with assisting with and supporting a voluntary treatment plan, is likely the better approach for helping someone recovering from an addiction.

If you have a loved one struggling with Substance-Use Disorder, find a way to let them know they are truly loved. Not just for the parts of them that are deemed worthy, but for every single part of them that exists. All the parts.

In Jaime's passing, I have become a grief container. I find honor and direction, and I discover meaning in my life through my new work.

Jaime once told me I should write a book about his life. I responded by suggesting he should write his own book. I told him that if he let me write his story, I would write it from my own point of view and would need to know his secrets, neither of which he would really enjoy. He just laughed. He was always prescient

For more information and to obtain resources about Substance-Use Disorder please reach out to your local support center or contact SAMHSA's National Helpline, 1-800-662-HELP (4357) (also known as the Treatment Referral Routing Service), or TTY: 1-800-487-4889 is a confidential, free, 24-hour-a-day, 365-day-a-year, information service, in English and Spanish, for individuals and family members facing mental and/or substance use disorders. This service provides referrals to local treatment facilities, support groups, and community-based organizations. Also, visit the online treatment locator, or send your zip code via text message: 435748 (HELP4U) to find help near you.

SimplePractice
https://www.simplepractice.com/blog/substance-abuse-tough-love-or-compassion-in-recovery/

Acknowledgments

Many thanks to the editors of the following journals in which these poems first appeared:

Everyday Grief "In the Waiting Room", *Poetry Ink* Moonstone Arts Center's 30th Edition "At Birth is Mammalian Instinct, Infant Intensely Staring", and *Fresh From the Exhibition, Issue I* Words Faerie Press "Then, a little accident, Those Bits of You Falling Out of Box"

Credit: "You Can Blow Out a Candle, But You Can't Blow Out a Fire" borrows its title from a lyric in Peter Gabriel's song *Biko* — a line that has lingered with me for years. "Riding Shotgun" was inspired by the fiery Shawn Colvin tune, *Shotgun Down the Avalanche.*

I offer sincere appreciation to the Victoria Police Department and the BC Coroners Service for their professionalism and humanity during an impossible year. In 2018, the year Jaime died, Victoria's fentanyl mortality rate rose sharply. In a city of roughly ninety-two thousand people, ninety-eight lives were lost. In January alone, the month Jaime left us, one hundred and twenty people were hospitalized for fentanyl overdoses. These are not abstractions. They are more than numbers. They are sons and daughters, mothers and fathers, friends and lovers.

My gratitude to the Santa Fe Art Institute for a residency that offered more than space and time. The

Creative Access Fellowship became a small, steady flame at the end of a long, dark corridor. To my daily workshop companions — Janet, John, Sharon, Ali, Courtney, and Wes — thank you for showing up with your pages, your artwork, and your courage. Because of you, I was not alone in the room. Everyone at SFAI — even Judy Chicago smiling from the library wall — made the simple act of arriving a gesture toward healing. Thank you to Barb for Taos, and to Rebecca for helping braid together our shared, strange history.

My love and enduring thanks to Chris (Yeti) Springbett for his generous tribute, for shaping Jaime's biography with such tenderness, and for allowing me to carry your words into these pages. You were one of Jaime's most steadfast friends. When you left this world, the silence widened again. I like to imagine you and Jaime somewhere just beyond our reach, still making music together.

Thank you to Natalie Rae Geer for the luminous story of Jaime and the fireworks — a story that feels less like memory and more like metaphor. After he passed, more stories about fireworks surfaced.

I am deeply grateful to my poetry editors and give my thanks to the angels who led me to find such a talented and generous group of women. First, Lise Goett, whose own poetic work continues to instruct and elevate. Thank you for your patience, your clarity and your early encouragement. Your sweet words inspired me to carry on. Gratitude to Laurel Corona for your insightful reading and for helping me recognize that there were, in fact, two books waiting to be written. Phyllis Erickson, your long telephone editorial/ therapy sessions pushed the poems beyond their solitude toward something shared. Heather Derr-Smith, your generous and delicately detailed editorial letter arrived amid another heartbreak, the loss of Jaime's best friend, and when I'd found my mind again, I could not find your words. When I did, they were a healing balm and will be my ongoing poetic field guide. My heart thanks you. Michal "MJ" Jones, a beautiful writer, your lyric precision felt like alchemy — a careful, necessary refinement of what these pieces were reaching toward.

So much gratitude and awe to my sound producer, Jeremy Miller. You arrived relatively late to this project and just in time to bring this fever dream to its aural reality.

To my fellow writers in the Two Table Writing Group and Dreamers in the Heights — thank you for your constancy and your generous talents. Deep bows to the Maya Moon Collective in San Diego for space, coffee, chocolate, and the sweet permission to congregate and continue.

Special gratitude to Jann Nunn, whose sculptures gave birth to the creation she translated for the cover to my words. Her artistry became the veil this book required. And to Lorie (Miles) Tancredi-Baese for her thoughtful design eye in shaping the book's format, photography, and graphics. Both collaborations — both of your visual languages — carry what words cannot.

To our family — and Jaime's Canadian family, both chosen and biological — and to the extended circle of friends who shared stories, photographs, fragments of music, and memory: this book is braided from your offerings. Eight years in the making, it is a fusion of love.

To my dearest friends who refused to turn away from the horror of this loss — who stayed, who listened, who allowed grief to sit at the table without flinching — thank you for sheltering me when I could not stand on my own.

My lasting love and gratitude to Jo-El Hartman, Jaime's buddy, and other mother.

And finally — my deepest gratitude — and my most enduring love — is with Jaime, who carries both the weight of grief and the grace of forgiveness beside me.

Musician Bio

Critical (Jaime Yates) is an American/Canadian producer, DJ, and sound engineer whose work has moved through breaks, glitch hop, dubstep, and bass music for more than two decades. His posthumous release, *Never Letting Go*, includes hits spanning decades of his recording career.

He first gained notice through releases on the UK underground labels **Mechanoise** and **Waveshape Records**, earning vinyl distribution and, for his single *The Way I Feel*, airplay on BBC Radio One during Annie Nightingale's celebrated program — one of the longest-running and most influential shows in British electronic music broadcasting.

His track *Hype the Funk* was remixed by Calvertron and Tom EQ, and he appears on the Breakz R Boss Records compilation *Canadian Breakbeat Classics 2000–2010.*

Critical's remix of M.E.L.T. reached number one on the TrackItDown Dubstep chart, and he has received support from DJs including Afghan Headspin, Reso, Reid Speed, Nom de Strip, and Peo De Pitte.

Working in partnership with fellow Canadian producer Beatsmith, Critical contributed guest mixes to The Crystal Method's radio program *Community Service* — broadcast on SiriusXM and Indie 103.1 — performing an appearance on which the duo played their own work alongside music from across the electronic canon. The Crystal Method personally introduced them to the program's international audience. Critical and Beatsmith's collaborative recordings have been released through The Pooty Club Records and, most recently, through DistroKid.

Critical's catalog has appeared on labels across four continents, including DistroKid, Breakz R Boss Records, The PootyClub Records, Nu Industry Recordings, Dusted Breaks, and Elektroshok Records in Spain, where he also toured and collaborated with local artists. Critical's track "The Way I Feel" received airplay on commercial radio in Spain. His work continues to receive radio and music festival play worldwide.

In 2016, Jaime received a full scholarship for music production at **Nimbus School of Recording & Media**. In 2017, his professional work as a sound engineer included contributions to *Gears of War*, the video game franchise developed by Epic Games, and published by **Microsoft,** where he worked on the audio production of one of the medium's most widely played series.

You can find Jaime's (Critical) music online on various music distribution sites, including Apple Music, YouTube, iTunes, Spotify, SoundCloud, Beatport, Anghami, MediaNet, Kuack Media, Boomplay, Saavn, Pandora, Flo, Jooks, Tidal, Tencent, Claro Música, iHeartRadio, Qubuz, Shazam, and Deezer. Tracks are also available for streaming on SoundCloud (**@criticalbc**).

Author Bio

J. Dylan Yates' work includes the award-winning novel, *THE BELIEF IN Angels.* Dylan's poetry has appeared in numerous journals and anthologies, including *Grief Like Yours: A Story Collection of Life After Loss*, *A Year in Ink*, *Volume 10*, *The Word Faire,* and *Moonstone Arts' 30th Edition of Poetry Ink.*

Dylan is an RN, Certified Grief Support Specialist, and Thanatologist. She holds a BFA from the University of Colorado-Boulder.

For more info: www.jdylanyates.com

Artist Bios

Best known for her work in sculpture, California-based artist **Jann Nunn** has exhibited, lectured, and held residencies internationally and throughout the United States since 1987. Nunn's work is in numerous public and private collections.

She studied art at the University of Alaska Anchorage, the Skowhegan School of Painting and Sculpture in Maine, the San Francisco Art Institute, and is Professor Emeritus of Sculpture at Sonoma State University.

For more information, please visit www.jann.nunn.com

Lorie Tancredi-Baese is a published artist and photography instructor with 23 years of experience at the School of Creative and Performing Arts. Currently teaching at San Diego State University (SDSU), she has been featured in various group and solo exhibitions. Lorie is a graduate of Art Center College of Design in Pasadena.

For more information, please visit www.lbaese.com

www.ingramcontent.com/pod-product-compliance
Lightning Source LLC
LaVergne TN
LVHW011048110826
845149LV00015B/3408

* 9 7 8 0 9 9 6 3 8 2 5 5 7 *